FIRST SEDER, LAST SUPPER

LAST SUPPER

AN INTERFAITH HAGGADAH

A celebration of Passover and Easter
Alison & David Lewis Stein

In memoriam
Rev. Paul Fairley

For information address the authors,
153 Daniel Street North,
Arnprior, ON. Canada K7S 2L2

Clink Street Publishing
1 Clink St.
London SE1 9DG
United Kingdom

ISBN 978-1-909477-48-3

1. Seder – Interfaith
2. Dialogue – Jewish/Christian
3. Liturgy – Jewish/Christian service

In preparing First Seder/Last Supper we read the Haggadah's mentioned
in our acknowledgements. We would not wish to imply that these
authors would support what we have written but we appreciate the work
they have done.

Preface

Why is this Haggadah different from all other Haggadahs?

Hundreds of prayer books have been written for Passover, each one undoubtedly a little different from all the ones that went before. Celebrations of Passover go back over 3,000 years and they are still changing and evolving.

This Haggadah is about sharing.

The Seder, the Passover feast, is an exciting, joyful event.

Jews often invite those who are not Jewish to join them in commemorating the night that God passed over Egypt and Moses led the Israelite slaves to freedom.

Many churches include a Seder in their Holy Week observances because when Christ came to Jerusalem for the last time, he told his followers to find a place where they could mark the Passover.

The authors of this Haggadah believe we are growing into a time when Jews and Christians can talk openly to each other. They can even sometimes marry each other.

But can they pray together?

That is the question inspiring this Haggadah.

Raising questions and then challenging the answers is a time honored Passover tradition.

Can people who want to live side by side in creative harmony achieve more than expressions of acceptance and good will?

How far can Jews and Christians go hand in hand?

Where are the borders? Where are the roads that Jews and Christians cannot travel together?

If Jews and Christians must always in the end go their separate ways, how separate are they?

These questions move though this Haggadah.

We hope people will turn to the notes and explanations at the back and then use this Haggadah with a spirit of discovery.

CONDUCTOR

Tonight we gather around this table to celebrate with food and drink, with questions and answers, with music, song and laughter, amazing events that wind around each other at the core of two great religions.
We begin with the liberation of the Jewish slaves from the bondage of slavery and we remember the days of Jesus in Galilee. Sheheckeyanu!
In Hebrew that means we are thanking the Creator who has supported us, protected us and brought us to this time and place.
Let us all say together, Sheheckeyanu!

ALL

Sheheckeyanu! Sheheckeyanu!

שההחינו

CONDUCTOR

People with candles in front of them please light
them now and we will all say:

ALL

May the flames we kindle here tonight help us stand together.
May the fires of creation illuminate our lives.

CONDUCTOR

We will do many things together tonight
so let's begin by saying hello to each other.

*(For example, "I am David, Zayde (Grandfather in Yiddish) Stein, husband and helper to
Alison and tonight I get to be a temporary big shot, the conductor of the service."
If someone has been designated to lead the musical portions,
the conductor should turn to him next…
"And on my left"…going around the table…
Or, "I am Alison Stein, Nana Stein, wife to David Stein, and
tonight I am the conductor of our Seder service."
You can have one person lead the whole service or break it up with different
people reading different sections. Or you can go around the room with each
person reading a line or two…whatever feels best at the time.)*

CONDUCTOR

We begin with the age-old question:
Why is this night different from all other nights?

CONDUCTOR AND PARTICIPANTS (SINGING OR CHANTING)

Mah nishtanah ha laylah hazeh mikol halaylot?

מה נשתנה הלילה הזה מכל הלילות

CONDUCTOR

There are many answers but tonight let us all say together:

ALL

This night is different because Jews believe that on this night God, not an
angel, not an archangel but the living God passed over Egypt leading the
Israelites out of slavery and on to Mount Sinai and there, in the midst
of thunder and lightning, God delivered the ten commandments that
became the core of Judaism.

This night is different because Christians believe that on this night Jesus celebrated the Passover with his disciples, a last supper before he was betrayed and crucified, and rose from the dead and on this night Jesus gave his disciples teachings that became the Eucharist, the sacred core of Christianity.

CONDUCTOR

We will now say Kiddush, the blessing over the first glass of wine. During the Seder we will drink four glasses of wine in remembrance of the four ways in which the Creator helped the Israelite slaves: the Creator freed them from slavery… led them out of Egypt… protected them and blessed them.

The four glasses of wine stand too for the four gospels that brought the news of Christ's mission in the world, the stories told by Matthew, Mark, Luke and John.

(Some people prefer to use grape juice or some other fruit juice rather than wine. There is nothing mandatory about the use of wine. What is important is that there be enough of whatever beverage is used to accompany the four blessings that are pronounced during the evening.)

ALL
Blessed is God who brings forth fruit from the vine.

ברוך אתה יי אלהינו מלך העולם בורא פרי הגפן

CONDUCTOR AND THOSE WHO WISH TO SAY THE HEBREW BLESSING

Baruch ata Adonai Eloheynu meleck haolam boray p'ri hagafen.

PARTICIPANT

I'm getting hungry. Can't we just eat and get on with it?

Patience...we do this for the four eternally questioning children of the Seder...and for the child in all of us.

PARTICIPANT

The angry Jewish child asks:
How can we celebrate Passover with people
who persecuted us for centuries?

PARTICIPANT

The militant Christian child asks:
How can we pray with people who do not
acknowledge the divinity of Christ?

PARTICIPANT

The skeptical child asks:
Why all these rituals when you cannot prove that God,
or The Creator, or whatever you want to call it, even exists?

PARTICIPANT

The disbelieving child asks:
Why waste your time praying?
There is no God.
Go out and build a better world.

CONDUCTOR

To the angry Jewish child we say:
We cannot take you into the past and exact revenge on persecutors.
But in our time you can reach out to others and work for a
future free from bigotry and persecution.

To the militant Christian child we say:
Throughout history there have been people who talked to God.
They called this divinity by many names:
Adonai, Baal, Krishna, Ahura Mazda, Ra, Zeus, Jesus, Odin, Manitou, Allah...
Do not presume to know where all the prayers of all these millions of people
have gone to. Let it be enough for you to pray in the way you know best and
seek your own salvation.

To the skeptical child we say:
You cannot prove to us that God does not exist,
just as we cannot prove to you that God is here, living among us.
But by celebrating with us, you at least hold yourself open to the possibility
of experiencing the Divine.
And you never know...strange and wonderful
things might happen to you tonight.

To the disbelieving child we say:
The great social movements to make a better world began with people of
faith reaching out to shelter the homeless, feed the hungry and free the slaves.
By celebrating Easter and Passover with us tonight you honor their memory.
You show yourself ready to carry on their good work.

ALL SING

I went out one morning and what did I see?
Four mighty birds in four mighty trees
And they sang to me, and they sang to me

The first sang of light at the start of the day
The next sang of work and bustle and pay
And they sang to me, and they sang to me

The third sang of night, of love and of play
The last sang of dreams that lighten the way
And they sang to me, and they sang to me

And I said, we have waited forever and ever
For you to sing your songs together
And they sang to me, and they sang to me

We must stay in these trees, this is where we belong
But for you all our voices may join in one song
And they sang to me, and they sang to me

One mighty song, one mighty song
To lift me up, carry me along.
-Alison, David and Benjamin Stein

Please see music notation at the back of this Haggadah

Conductor

Behold these three matzah.
They stand for three ways in which all Christian Churches are divided:
the hierarchy, the clergy and the laity.

These three pieces stand for the three divisions among the Jewish people:
the Cohens, who were the priesthood, the Levites who were the servants and
guardians of the temple in Jerusalem, and the B'nai Yisroel,
the children of Israel.

*(The leader takes the middle board of matzah, breaks it in half and, if there are children present,
explains that this is the "Afikoman." He is going to hide the Afikoman and the children will hunt
for it at the end of the meal. The one who finds it can claim a reward...money or a sweet.)*

Participant

On the night the Jewish slaves were finally able to leave Egypt
there was no time to let the bread dough rise.
The fleeing slaves carried the dough on their backs and the
sun baked it into the wafers we still consume at Passover.
When we bite into this matzah, the hard bread of affliction,
we remember the needy people in our midst.
Let all who are hungry join our Seder meal.

Participant

Aren't we being just a bit hypocritical here, talking as though all the
hungry people in the world could crowd around this Seder table?

Participant

Would it not be even worse if we went on with our feast as though we didn't
know some people are starving out there?

Participant

God warned the Jews that they were not leaving the poor behind
when they left Egypt, the poor would always be with them.
They should always be fair and just to those in need.

PARTICIPANT

The apostle Paul said to the Christian congregation in Corinth, "Though I speak with the tongues of men and of angels, and have not charity, I am become as sounding brass or a tinkling cymbal."

PARTICIPANT

Paul meant more than giving from the wallet and giving from the purse, charity means giving from the heart. Helping others is an act of love.

"Three things endure," Paul told the Corinthians, "Faith, hope and love, but the greatest of these is love."

PARTICIPANT

The Torah instructs Jews to tithe, devote one tenth of all they earn, to helping others.

PARTICIPANT

Jews are also told to leave the corners of their fields unharvested so that widows and orphans can reap grain there and live.

PARTICIPANT

Charity, Tzedakah in Hebrew, is considered one of the greatest Mitzvahs, good deeds, a Jew can perform.
Tzedakah means more than generosity.
Tzedakah is doing justice, giving to the poor the share that is their due.

The prophet Micah said that what is required of us is to do justice, love mercy and walk humbly with our God.

PARTICIPANT

One day Jesus told his disciples to feed the crowd that had come to hear him but the disciples found they had only a basket with five loaves of bread and two fishes.

PARTICIPANT

The disciples must have been very fearful. When they ran out of food would the hungry crowd grow angry and attack them?

PARTICIPANT

Jesus told the disciples to begin distributing this meager ration and to their amazement, they found there was enough food to go around.

PARTICIPANT

The late Reverend Paul Fairley, to whom this Haggadah is dedicated, used to say the miracle of the loaves and fishes was that people put food into the basket as it was passed around as well as taking food out, so that all were fed.

Let each of us put into the spiritual basket of this mixed Jewish and Christian celebration as much as we can share with others…and take out of it as much as we can draw into our own lives.

PARTICIPANT

When do we get to eat? Couldn't we have less talk and more food?

PARTICIPANT

We are about to start.
But you must know that we are not just consuming a meal to commemorate the liberation of Hebrew slaves.

PARTICIPANT

I knew it! More talk.

CONDUCTOR

In the traditional Seder when the wise son asks why we
perform all these rituals, he is told we do all this
because of what God did <u>for me</u> when I left Egypt.
So tonight we are celebrating what God did <u>for us</u> when we left Egypt.
We are reliving chapters of our common history.

PARTICIPANT

Tonight we are all slaves fleeing Egypt with bundles of unleavened bread dough on our backs.

PARTICIPANT

Tonight we are the liberated Jews at Mt. Sinai listening to Moses deliver the Ten Commandments.

PARTICIPANT

Tonight we are all farmers and fishermen and tax collectors in Galilee listening to Jesus preaching the beatitudes.

PARTICIPANT

Tonight we are among the awestruck crowds in Jerusalem watching Jesus hang from the cross.

CONDUCTOR

We open our Seder meal with karpas… a green herb (parsley, or some other vegetable or even a piece of fruit such as a strawberry) and an egg. The egg and green herb come from eternal renewal rising out of the earth.

On other nights we may dip our herbs in salt water only once, on Passover we dip them twice: the first time we dip our herbs in salt water because we remember the tears that were shed by the Jewish slaves and by the early Christian martyrs. We dip our herbs a second time in salty water in honor of the tears that have been shed by all those who have suffered for their faith.

(The conductor points to objects on the Seder plate and explains their significance. Other participants may have similar Seder plates in front of them and they can point to objects as the speaker mentions them.)

CONDUCTOR

The animal bone honors the sacrificial lambs whose blood was spread on Jewish door posts so God could recognize the homes of people to be spared. And it recognizes those who believe that Jesus was himself a sacrificial lamb whose death could redeem the world.

Now please put a bit of this maror, horseradish, on a piece of matzah, and bite into it. That is the bitter taste of slavery. Now put a bit of this charoseth (a mixture of apples, nuts and honey) on a piece of matzah. That is the sweet taste of liberation and happiness. Hillel, a great sage who lived at the time of Jesus, used to mix charoseth and maror on a piece of matzah…as we all should be doing now…to remind ourselves at Passover that bitterness and happiness are mixed together in all our lives.[1]

PARTICIPANT

What is that orange doing on the Seder plate?

CONDUCTOR

The story is told that a woman once asked a very narrowminded, observant Rabbi what place women have at the Bimah, the synagogue lectern where the Torah is read. The strict rabbi replied that women belong at the Bimah the way an orange belongs on the Seder plate. Tonight we place an orange on our Seder plate.

---

1 Centuries before the Earl of Sandwich ordered a waiter to bring him a slice of beef between two slices of bread so he could eat without interrupting his card game and gave his name to a staple of our diet, Rabbi Hillel mixed horseradish and charoseth between two pieces of Matzoh. If history had unrolled differently, there might now be "Hillel shops" scattered around the world instead of sandwich shops. A lame joke perhaps, but it does illustrate how the course of our lives can twist and turn. For thousands of years Jews were outsiders living in other people's countries. But their history began in a country of their own.
It's been said that if ancient Israel had not been conquered by the Assyrians, the Babylonians and the Greeks and if the Romans had not destroyed the temple in Jerusalem and scattered the Israelites through their empire, the Jewish people might now be as numerous as the Chinese people. Sometimes thinking about the world that might have been can help us see more clearly the world that is.

PARTICIPANT

So many stories. Why do we keep telling stories?

PARTICIPANT

It was the opinion of Rabbi Nachman that God
made the world because he loves stories.[1]

PARTICIPANT

Rabbi Akiva, a shepherd who became a renowned first century scholar and
authority on Jewish law, used to say that the person who does not tell the
story of the Exodus at the Seder has not fulfilled the obligations of Passover.

ALL SING

We love to tell the Story
For those who know it best
Seem hungering and thirsting
To hear it, like the rest.
And when, in scenes of glory,
We sing the new, new song,
"Twill be — the old, old story
That we have loved so long.
- 19th Century Gospel Hymn

Please see music notation at the back of this Haggadah

1 Rabbi Nachman of Breslau was an early Hassidic master. Hassidim were followers of the Baal Shem Tov, master of the Good Name [of God], an 18th century teacher who sought to give music and dance and mystical experiences a more prominent place in Jewish religious observance. Hassidic rebbes, teachers, made it a practice to live among the people. The closest analogy would be Catholic worker priests.

The story of the exodus begins when Moses, an Egyptian prince
comes upon an overseer beating one of the Jewish slaves
building monuments to the Pharaoh.

But Moses is himself a Jew, a descendant of the 70 Jews an earlier
Pharaoh had welcomed into Egypt during a time of famine.

Moses' ancestor, Joseph, had supervised the storing of food for seven
prosperous years so that the Egyptians could survive the seven
lean years Joseph had foreseen.

Joseph was the second youngest of Jacob's twelve sons.
He was the grandson of Isaac and the great grandson of Abraham
who first heard the call of the One God.

Abraham had led his family to Canaan and had began a conversation with the
One God that opened the history of the Jewish people.

Abraham's grandson, Jacob, favored Joseph, the dreamer, over all his other
sons. Joseph's brothers grew envious. They seized Joseph and sold him into
slavery in Egypt. But Joseph rose from a prison cell to save Egypt from famine.
Joseph became a civil servant in Egypt, second in
power only to Pharaoh himself.

When refugees come to our door asking for shelter we should remember
how much Joseph, the refugee and exile, did for the people of Egypt.

For many generations the Jews lived peacefully among the Egyptians.
But there came a Pharaoh who knew not Joseph.

This new Pharaoh feared the Jews would dilute the purity of Egyptian blood and conspire with his enemies. Step by step the Pharaoh curtailed the freedom of the Israelites and turned them finally into slaves.

When we remember Pharaoh driving the Israelites out of the lives they had built up over hundreds of years among the Egyptians, we think of Hitler and the Nazis, Stalin and the chain of slave labor camps in Siberia, Pol Pot and the Khmer Rouge atrocities in Cambodia…and all the rulers we have seen in our own time turn against their own people and of all the neighbors we have seen turn against neighbors.

Pharaoh became so fearful that he ordered midwives to kill every male Jewish child as soon as the child was born. Two heroic midwives defied Pharaoh and saved the son of Yocheved. Yocheved placed the baby in a basket and floated the basket down the Nile. Pharaoh's daughter had come to the river to bathe. She spied the basket and drew it out of the water. She decided to raise the baby as her own child.[1]

1 Women of all classes in the Exodus story are named — an extraordinary practice in ancient times. So we know that the midwives who saved countless Hebrew babies were, Shifra and Puah, that the mother of Moses was Yocheved and his sister was Miriam. Miriam became a prophet herself and it is said she led the Israelites to water during their long trek through the desert. The story is told that God spoke directly to the Egyptian princess and told her that because she had loved this child of slavery as though Moses were her own son, God would call her 'My daughter.' Thus she was Batya or 'The daughter of God.'

Moses grew up in the Pharaoh's household, a prince of Egypt, but one day he saw a brutal overseer attacking a Jewish slave. This Jewish Egyptian prince threw himself between them and ended by killing the Egyptian overseer.

Moses had to flee to the land of Midian where he became a shepherd.

Moses was out in the desert with his flock when he saw a bush that was burning but was not being consumed. Moses was amazed, but God spoke to Moses from the midst of the flames. God directed Moses to tell the Israelite slaves that their God, "I Am That I Am" had heard their groaning and understood their suffering. God told Moses to go before Pharaoh with his brother, Aaron, and demand that Pharaoh free the slaves.

Pharaoh would not listen to Moses and Aaron.
With scorn and contempt Pharaoh turned them away.
And so God brought down plagues upon Egypt…blood
filling the River Nile…swarms of frogs everywhere…
an infestation of lice biting all living creatures…
wild beasts trampling the fields…cattle disease…
painful boils that sickened people…hail storms flatten-
ing crops…clouds of ravenous locusts devouring everything in their path…darkness covering the land.

ALL SING

When Israel was in Egypt land
Let my people go
Oppressed so hard they could not stand
Let my people go.
Go down Moses
Way down in Egypt Land
Tell ol' Pharaoh
Let my people go.
So God told Moses what to do,
Let my people go
To lead his people right on through
Let my people go.
Go down, Moses etc.
When Israel reached the water side
Let my people go
Commanded God,
"It shall divide"
Let my people go.
Go down Moses etc.
--African American spiritual

Please see music notation at the back of this Haggadah

After every plague, Moses and Aaron went before
Pharaoh and begged Pharaoh to free the slaves.
Each time Pharaoh scorned them and turned his back on them.

We remember what the Jewish slaves suffered and
we should remember too what the Egyptian people suffered.
What did the Egyptians think when their crops were destroyed by hail stones
and locusts, when their cattle fell ill and when the Nile River they depended
on to irrigate their land so they could grow their crops turned to blood? We
know only that Pharaoh called in his own priests and wise men and they used
all their knowledge and all their magic and they could not stop the plagues.
But still Pharaoh would not listen to Moses.
Tonight when we are trying to enter into the suffering of the Israelite slaves,
we should remember too the suffering of ordinary Egyptians.
They were not slave drivers.
They were just trying to get on with their lives but they were being made to
suffer because of Pharaoh's arrogance.

How often in our own time have we witnessed people suffering because of
the arrogance of their rulers?

CONDUCTOR

At this table we might ask of ourselves how much do we
share in responsibility and guilt for what our leaders sometimes do?

** A cautionary note to the conductor: this could initiate an interesting and
fruitful discussion but try to keep it focussed and bring it to conclusion.
Remember, dinner is waiting!*

CONDUCTOR

Finally, God calls down the most terrible plague of all, death of the firstborn. Moses warns the Israelites to sacrifice a lamb and smear blood on their
door posts. Then God passes over Egypt sparing Jewish homes but slaying the
firstborn of the Egyptians.

When Pharaoh sees his people losing their children and suffering in the way
he has made the Jewish slaves suffer, he finally lets the slaves go free.

ALL

We hope for a time when nations will not have to pass through times of
oppression and violence before their rulers learn to act with compassion.

PARTICIPANTS

Pharaoh's own experience of compassion does not last. Pharaoh sends an
army to drag the Israelites back to slavery.
The army catches up with them just as they reach the Red Sea.
The Israelites are terrified.
Has Moses led them out of Egypt only to bring them to death and destruction?
But the waters of the Red Sea fall back and the
fleeing slaves cross over on a corridor of dry land.
The furious Egyptian army charges in pursuit but the
waters return and roll back over them.
Then it is said the Angels in heaven began to sing and dance.
God rebuked the Angels saying, "How can you rejoice? The Egyptians are my
people too and these Egyptian soldiers are drowning."

When they get beyond the Red Sea the liberated slaves are overcome with gratitude. They begin to compose hymns thanking God for everything God has done for them and saying that each act of divine intervention would have been enough. "Dayenu!" It would have been enough.

CONDUCTOR

This is a good moment for us to have our second glass of wine and give thanks for things that enrich our lives.

(All fill their second glass of wine and say:)

Le Chayim! To life! Le Chayim! Le Chayim! To Life!

לחיים ~ לחיים

CONDUCTOR

I will enumerate some of these experiences. Others may wish to add things we are grateful for. After each one, let us all sing the chorus of thanksgiving.

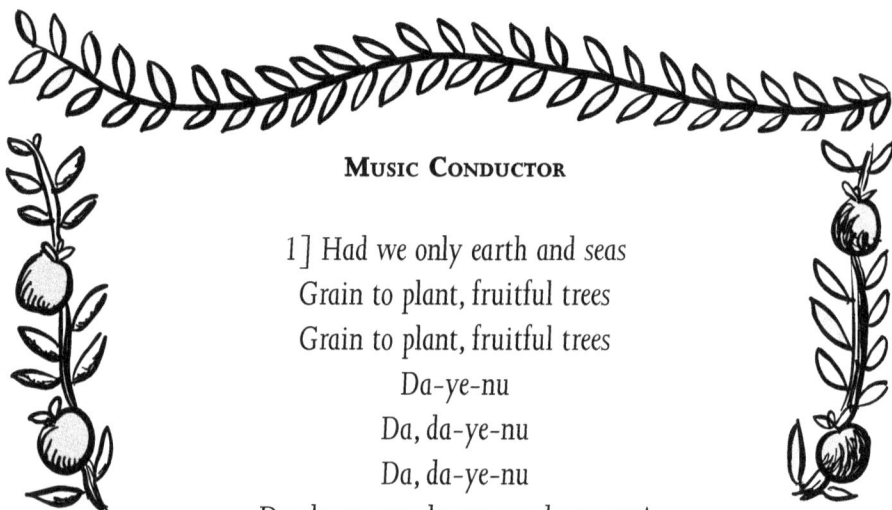

MUSIC CONDUCTOR

1] *Had we only earth and seas*
Grain to plant, fruitful trees
Grain to plant, fruitful trees
Da-ye-nu
Da, da-ye-nu
Da, da-ye-nu
Da, da-ye-nu, da-ye-nu, da-ye-nu!

2] Could we scan the books on shelves
And never learn to see ourselves
Never come to see ourselves
Da-ye-nu
Da, da-ye-nu
Da, da-ye-nu
Da, da-ye-nu, da-ye-nu, da-ye-nu!

3] Could we feel the power of love
But never reach for stars above
Never reach for stars above
Da-ye-nu
Da, da-ye-nu
Da, da-ye-nu
Da, da-ye-nu, da-ye-nu, da-ye-nu!

4] Could we only banish sorrow
Wipe our tears, face tomorrow
Wipe our tears, face tomorrow
Da-ye-nu
Da, da-ye-nu
Da, da-ye-nu
Da, da-ye-nu, da-ye-nu, da-ye-nu!

5] Could we only raise our voices
Join our hands, share our choices
Join our hands, share our choices
Da-ye-nu
Da, da-ye-nu
Da, da-ye-nu
Da, da-ye-nu, da-ye-nu, da-ye-nu!
-Traditional tune

Please see music notation at the back of this Haggadah

We will now say together the prayer that Aaron, the brother of Moses, taught the high priests as the Jews began their long walk into the desert.

All

May God bless you and keep you
May the grace of God sustain you
May God's radiance shine upon you
and give you peace.

Conductor

Several hundred years later Jesus, the son of a carpenter in Nazareth,
began to preach in Galilee.
He speaks of purifying souls and of love among people.

Participant

At the little town of Cana Jesus performs his first miracle.
People are celebrating a wedding but they have run out of wine and the family are afraid they will be humiliated in front of guests.
Mary, the mother of Jesus, asks him to help.
He turns water into wine and the wedding celebration goes on.

Participant

Jesus roams across Judea teaching and performing miracles.
A blind man receives the power to see. People with twisted bodies are cured and made whole. A crippled man is bought before Jesus on a bed.
Jesus tells him to get up.
The man who had been crippled stands up and
walks away carrying the bed with him.

In the midst of a terrible storm, Jesus walks on the Sea of Galilee to reach a boat that is carrying his disciples. Suddenly the storm dies down. The water becomes calm.

Crowds begin to gather around Jesus.
The lessons in the stories he tells, the parables,
are as demanding as debates in the Talmud.

PARTICIPANT

Jesus comes across a crowd about to stone to death a
woman who has been caught committing adultery. Jesus
tells them that the person who has never committed a
sin in his life should cast the first stone. One by one the
crowd disperses and Jesus is left alone with the woman.
He tells the woman to go and sin no more.

PARTICIPANT

Is Jesus telling us that only people who are totally free
of sin can be police officers? Who should the judges
be? If only people pure of heart can administer justice,
where will all the lawyers go?

PARTICIPANT

Jesus tells of a man attacked by robbers,
beaten and left bleeding on the road. Travelers cross to
the other side. At last a Samaritan, an outsider, comes
upon the bleeding man. He binds his wounds, takes
him to an inn and pays for the
innkeeper to care for him.

PARTICIPANT

But what if the innkeeper fails in this task? Should the
Samaritan have made certain the wounded
man got safely home?

When we undertake to help someone at a difficult time do we become responsible for that person? Are there limits to the help we are called upon to give? How do we set such limits?

A place for discussion *

PARTICIPANT

Jesus tells of a rich man's son who demands his inheritance and then spends it all in riotous living. Very quickly the boy has nothing left. He returns home and tells his father he is no longer worthy to be his son. But instead of demanding an apology the father kills a fatted calf and holds a great feast to welcome the prodigal home.

PARTICIPANT

If the father does not punish the son, if the father does not even demand an
apology, how can the father be sure his son will not go off again
and become destructive?

PARTICIPANT

If someone has wronged us should we demand an apology and a promise
never to do it again before we offer help? Or can we, like the father of the
prodigal son, show love without asking anything in return.
Can we show unconditional love?

PARTICIPANT

The Roman army of occupation and their collaborators among the Jewish
authorities began to fear that Jesus would incite the people to rebellion.
They send an agent to trap Jesus into speaking treason.

PARTICIPANT

Teacher, do you believe in paying taxes?

PARTICIPANT

Jesus tells the agent to hold up a coin. "Whose face is on the coin?" Jesus asks.
"Caesar's face," the agent says.

PARTICIPANT

"Then render unto Caesar what is Caesar's. And render unto God what is God's."

PARTICIPANT

But what if Caesar keeps borrowing and running up the public debt? What if Caesar never allows a tax cut?

PARTICIPANT

Jesus and his followers come to Jerusalem to celebrate the Passover. He enters the city riding on a donkey. His fame has spread and joyful crowds line the streets. Jesus tells his disciples to find a place where they can celebrate the Passover.

PARTICIPANT

When they settle down for the Passover meal, Jesus takes a piece of bread…matzah…breaks it and says to his disciples, "This is my body which is broken for you. When you do this, remember me."

PARTICIPANT

Jesus takes the wine and says, "This is my blood, which is shed for you. When you drink this, remember me." Then he offers the bread and wine to his disciples.

Jesus leads his disciples to the garden of Gethsemane and asks them to keep watch while he goes apart and prays. When he returns he finds the disciples he had asked to keep watch have fallen asleep.
"The spirit is willing but the flesh is weak," Jesus says ruefully.
A mob led by Roman soldiers comes searching for Jesus. Judas Iscariot, one of his disciples, kisses Jesus to identify him. Jesus is seized and put on trial.

PARTICIPANT

Jesus is condemned to be crucified.

PARTICIPANT

For centuries, there were those who held the Jewish people responsible.
They said, "The Jews killed Christ."

PARTICIPANT

But Jesus Christ himself is a Jew. His disciples are all Jews.
His early followers are Jews.

PARTICIPANT

It is fear that killed Jesus.

PARTICIPANT

Fear of people making their own choices.

PARTICIPANT

Fear of people choosing their own leaders.

PARTICIPANT

Fear of people deciding when they will love and whom they will love.

CONDUCTOR

It has been said that all those corroded with envy of their neighbor's success, all the failed dreamers who cursed God for making a real world, and all the disappointed lovers who cursed those who spurned them — all these failed, bitter angry people came together at one time and in one place, and they conspired to crucify Jesus.

ALL SING

Were you there when they nailed him to the tree?
Were you there when they nailed him to the tree?
Oh, sometimes it causes me to tremble...tremble...tremble.
Were you there when they nailed him to the tree?

Were you there when they laid him in the tomb?
Were you there when they laid him in the tomb?
Oh, sometimes it causes me to tremble...tremble...tremble.
Were you there when they laid him in the tomb?
-African American traditional

Please see music notation at the back of this Haggadah

God will be with you.
When you go through rivers of difficulty you will not drown.
When you walk through the fire of oppression you will not
be burned up, the flames will not consume you.
-Isaiah. 43:2

PARTICIPANT

This is a terrifying time for the people of Judea. The Romans run a savage empire. They begin to attack and murder followers of Jesus, sometimes even throwing them to wild animals.
Lions tearing people apart make an entertaining spectacle for the mob in the Roman coliseum.

PARTICIPANT

Jews know only too well the terror those early followers of Jesus experience. Many times in their history Jews have suffered pogroms, political leaders setting mobs to attack and murder them.

PARTICIPANT

The followers of Jesus place his body in a cave and roll a gigantic stone in front of it. They want to make sure the body of
Jesus will never be disturbed.

PARTICIPANT

But that is not the end of the story.
When the disciples came back three days later the stone had been rolled back
and the body of Jesus had disappeared.

PARTICIPANT

For Christians this is the greatest moment of their history.
They say Christ has risen.
They say Jesus reigns now with God in heaven.

PARTICIPANT

Jews say: We cannot go there with you.
Jews say: God reigns alone. God is one. *Adonai echod.* God is indivisible.

PARTICIPANT

Is this where we stop?

PARTICIPANT

Have we spent all this time retelling stories and reliving histories we share
only to throw up our hands in the end and walk away from each other?

PARTICIPANT

Will we never get beyond the times when we have been enemies?

PARTICIPANT

Hear what the prophet Isaiah said:
"If your enemy is hungry, give them bread to eat.
If your enemy is thirsty, give them water to drink."

PARTICIPANT

God said to the Israelites in the desert, "You shall love your neighbor
as you love yourself."

PARTICIPANT

Jesus said to his disciples, "In everything, do to others as you
would have them do to you."

The Apostle Paul said in a letter to Galatians, that all the Law is fulfilled in that one statement, "You shall love your neighbor as yourself."

The 18ᵗʰ century thinker, Immanuel Kant, said in his Critique of Pure Reason, one should never treat another person as a means to an end but treat all persons as ends in themselves.

PARTICIPANT

A Roman soldier came to Hillel, the sage, and ordered him to explain the meaning of Judaism while the soldier was standing on one foot.

"Whatever is hateful to you, do not do that to other people. That is the heart of the Jewish religion," Hillel said. "All the rest is commentary. Now good soldier, go and study."

ALL SING

Hope is the answer.
Love is the way
To build the bridge
We have started today

The road may be long
But we won't be defeated.
We'll treat the whole world
as we would be treated

Hope is the answer.
Love is the way
To build the bridge
We have started today.

-Alison, David and Benjamin Stein

Please see music notation at the back of this Haggadah

CONDUCTOR

At Mt. Sinai God told the liberated slaves what was expected of
them and how to live in peace with their neighbors.
We will say together now the Ten Commandments:

ALL

1) I AM YOUR GOD WHO BROUGHT YOU OUT OF THE LAND OF EGYPT.
YOU SHALL NOT WORSHIP OTHER GODS BEFORE ME.

2) YOU SHALL NOT MAKE GRAVEN IMAGES AND BOW DOWN TO THEM.

3) YOU SHALL NOT TAKE THE NAME OF THE CREATOR IN VAIN,
UTTERING IT IN BLASPHEMY AND CURSES.

4) YOU SHALL REMEMBER THE SABBATH AND KEEP IT AS A HOLY DAY AND A DAY OF REST.

5) YOU SHALL HONOR YOUR FATHER AND YOUR MOTHER.

6) YOU SHALL NOT KILL.

7) YOU SHALL NOT COMMIT ADULTERY.

8) YOU SHALL NOT STEAL.

9) YOU SHALL NOT BEAR FALSE WITNESS AGAINST YOUR NEIGHBOR.

10) YOU SHALL NOT COVET YOUR NEIGHBOR'S POSSESSIONS.

On a hillside in Judea Jesus told his disciples how to
purify their inner, spiritual lives.
Let us say together the eight beatitudes:

ALL

Blessed are the poor in spirit for heaven belongs to them.
Blessed are the mourners for they shall be comforted.
Blessed are the meek for they shall inherit the earth.
Blessed are those who hunger for righteousness, they shall be satisfied.
Blessed are the merciful for they shall receive mercy.
Blessed are the pure of heart for they shall see God.
Blessed are the peacemakers for they shall be called the children of God.
Blessed are the ones, who suffer persecution for the sake of
righteousness, theirs is the kingdom of heaven.

CONDUCTOR

It is time now to begin our Passover feast.
We will say the blessing over our third glass of wine and begin our meal.

CONDUCTOR AND THOSE WHO WISH TO SAY THE HEBREW BLESSING

Blessed is the creator who brings forth fruit from the vine.

ברוך אתה יי אלהינו מלך העולם בורא פרי הגפן

Baruch ata Adonai Eloheynu meleck haolam boray p'ri hagafen..

לחיים ~ לחיים

Le Chayim! To life! Le Chayim!

We dedicate this meal to our hopes for the future.
We dream of a world at peace.
Before we start to eat, let us sing three times in Hebrew
a celebration of community.

Behold, how good and how pleasant it is for people
to dwell together in unity!

הנה מה טוב ומה נעים שבת אחים גם יחד

ALL SING

Hinei ma tov u'ma-nayim
Shevet ach-im gam ya-chad

Hinei ma tov u'ma-nayim
Shevet ach-im gam ya-chad

Hinei ma tov u'ma-nayim
Shevet ach-im gam ya-chad
- Traditional song

Please see music notation at the back of this Haggadah

The food is served.

We are coming to the end of our Seder meal and it is time for our fourth glass of wine. Let us say together:
Blessed is the Creator who brings forth fruit from the vine.

בָּרוּךְ אַתָּה יי אֱלֹהֵינוּ מֶלֶךְ הָעוֹלָם בּוֹרֵא פְּרִי הַגָּפֶן

Baruch ata Adonai Eloheynu meleck haolam boray p'ri hagafen.

לְחַיִּים ~ לְחַיִּים

Le Chayim! To life! Le Chayim!

Remember now what took place when the liberated Jewish slaves got to the end of their 40-year march through the desert.

Moses has come to the end of his long life and he knows that because of sins he has committed along the way, he himself will not be permitted to enter this land he has brought them to. He assembles the children of Israel on the banks of the river Jordan in sight of their new home and addresses them for the last time. Moses tells them that if they do not follow God's ways, terrible things may befall them. But they do have a choice. The future is up to them. "I have set before you this day life and death," Moses says. "Choose life."

Christians of different denominations say in Greek:
Kyrie Eleison
God have mercy

Jews say in Hebrew:
Chi layolam hass do
His mercy endures forever

CONDUCTOR

Before we say goodbye tonight, we will say these prayers together five times:
God have mercy
His mercy endures forever

PARTICIPANT

Why five times?

CONDUCTOR

Five for the fingers of the hand that reaches out to touch other hands. Please join hands with those close to you.

CONDUCTOR AND ALL

Kyrie Eleison…Chi layolam hass do
Kyrie Eleison …Chi layolam hass do
Kyrie Eleison…Chi layolam hass do
Kyrie Eleison…Chi layolam hass do
Kyrie Eleison…Chi layolam hass do

כי לעולם חסדו

PARTICIPANT

Have we answered the question we asked at the beginning?

PARTICIPANT

As the Passover feast draws to a close can we finally stand beside each other and pray to our different names for God?

PARTICIPANT

Can we join our divided hearts?

PARTICIPANT

Why not?
We're doing it aren't we?
Are we not all praying together?

PARTICIPANT

Here we go again!
Why does a Jew always answer a question by asking another question?

PARTICIPANT

Is it not all a question?

PARTICIPANT

In the end, isn't everything we know only the doorway to a mystery?

PARTICIPANT

Is that not what we all share in the end? A mystery?

CONDUCTOR

Let us join our voices together and say:

ALL

Amen. Le Chayim! To life! Le Chayim! Amen.

לחיים ~ לחיים

ALL SING

I'll sing you one-o
All sing together now.[1]

What is your one-o?

One for the One who made it all
One for the one who heard the call
Me for you and you for me
Singing all together[2]

I'll sing you two-o
All sing together now

What is your two-o?

Two, two the tablets
Two for the two great teachers[3]

---

1 Versions of this call and response song go back to the early Seders with "Who Knows One?`` "Echod mi Yodeah". This song continued on into medieval England with "Green Grow The Rushes Oh " and lives to this day. We hope participants in this Seder will add verses of their own - also songs of their own and make of this a joyful and memorable event.

2 We are taught that God made the world and the whole universe that we see around us. We are told that Abraham, the son of an idol maker in the ancient city of Ur, first heard the call of the one God and began the one God tradition of worship.

3 Moses, the prophet, carved the Ten Commandments onto two stone tablets and gave them to the Israelites at Mt Sinai. The apostle Paul drew the followers of Jesus together and began the Christian church.

One for the One who made it all
One for the one who heard the call
Me for you and you for me
Singing all together

I'll sing you three-o
All sing together now

What is your three-o?

Three, three the fathers
Three, three the trinity[1]

Two, two the tablets
Two for the two great teachers
One for the One who made it all
One for the one who heard the call
Me for you and you for me
Singing all together

I'll sing you four-o
All sing together now

What is your four-o?

Four for the gospel writers
Four for the four great mothers[2]

---

1 Abraham, Isaac and Jacob are the founding patriarchs of Judaism.
For Christians, God the father, Jesus the son and the Holy Spirit are the foundation stones of Christianity.
2 Mathew, Mark, Luke and John wrote the gospels, the story of Jesus' life.
Sarah, Rebecca, Rachel and Leah, the wives of Abraham, Isaac and Jacob, are the founding matriarchs of Judaism.

Three, three the fathers
Three, three the trinity
Two, two the tablets
Two for the two great teachers
One for the One who made it all
One for the one who heard the call
Me for you and you for me
Singing all together

I'll sing you five-o
All sing together now

What is your five-o?

Five for the books of Torah
Five for the five great saints[1]

Four for the gospel writers.
Four for the four great mothers.
Three, three the fathers
Three, three the trinity
Two, two the tablets
Two for the two great teachers
One for the One who made it all
One for the one who heard the call
Me for you and you for me
Singing all together

I'll sing you six-o
All sing together now

---

1 The five books of the Torah are the foundation stories of Judaism: Genesis, Exodus, Leviticus, Deuteronomy and Numbers. Augustine of Hippo, Thomas Aquinas, Patrick of Ireland, Hilda of Whitby and Francis of Assisi are among the outstanding early saints who formed the beginnings of Christianity.

What is your six-o?

Six for the days of making.
Six for the six great ages[1]

Five for the books of Torah
Five for the five great saints
Four for the gospel writers
Four for the founding mothers
Three, three the fathers
Three, three the trinity
Two, two the tablets
Two for the two great teachers
One for the One who made it all
One for the one who heard the call
Me for you and you for me
Singing all together

I'll sing you seven-o
All sing together now

What is your seven-o?

Seven for the day we all love best
Seven for the day we get to rest[2]

Six for the days of making
Six for the six great ages
Five for the books of Torah
Five for the five great saints
Four for the gospel writers
Four for the founding mothers

---

1 The Bible teaches us that God made the world in six days. Geologists measure six stages in the development of planet Earth: Hadean, Archeozoic Proterozoic, Paleozoic, Mesozoic and Cenozoic, the time in which we live out our lives.

2 In the ancient world, there was no established day of rest until the creation of the Jewish Sabbath.

Three, three the fathers
Three, three the trinity
Two, two the tablets
Two for the two great teachers
One for the One who made it all
One for the one who heard the call
Me for you and you for me
AND EVER MORE SHALL BE-O!
- Traditional folk song

Please see music notation at the back of this Haggadah

CONDUCTOR

We are nearing now the completion of our Passover celebration.
The authors of this Haggadah celebrated Passover Seders for many years with
the Ajzenstat family. We ended the evening, as many Seders do, by singing
Hatikvah, the Hebrew song of hope that has become the
national anthem of Israel. But one year, Sarah, the grandmother of the family,
said she had something to add. She had come from Poland in 1939, barely
escaping the Holocaust that engulfed the Jews of Europe, and going on to
raise a family in Canada. It was all very well to sing about Israel, Sarah said,
but she lives in Canada and Canada has allowed her to practise her religion
freely. Sarah asked us to sing the national anthem of Canada after we had sung
Hatikvah. And so we did.

ALL SING

O Canada, our home and native land
True patriot love in all of us command
With glowing hearts we see thee rise
The true north strong and free
From far and wide, O Canada
We stand on guard for thee
God keep our land, glorious and free
O Canada we stand on guard for thee
O Canada we stand on guard for thee

Please see music notation at the back of this Haggadah

(The authors suggest that if this Haggadah is being used in other countries of the diaspora and the celebrants feel the country where they reside has allowed them to practise their religion freely and live in peace, they sing the national anthem of the country they are in.)

The traditional Haggadah ending

It is traditional to end the Seder with the fervent wish
Next year in Jerusalem!
Jerusalem is a holy city for many faiths.
Let us build a holy city in our hearts and say together:

ALL

Le shannah habbah beeYerushalayim!
Next Year in Jerusalem!
Le shannah habbah beeYerushalayim!
Le shannah habbah beeYerushalayim!
Next year in Jerusalem!

לשנה הבאה בירושלים!

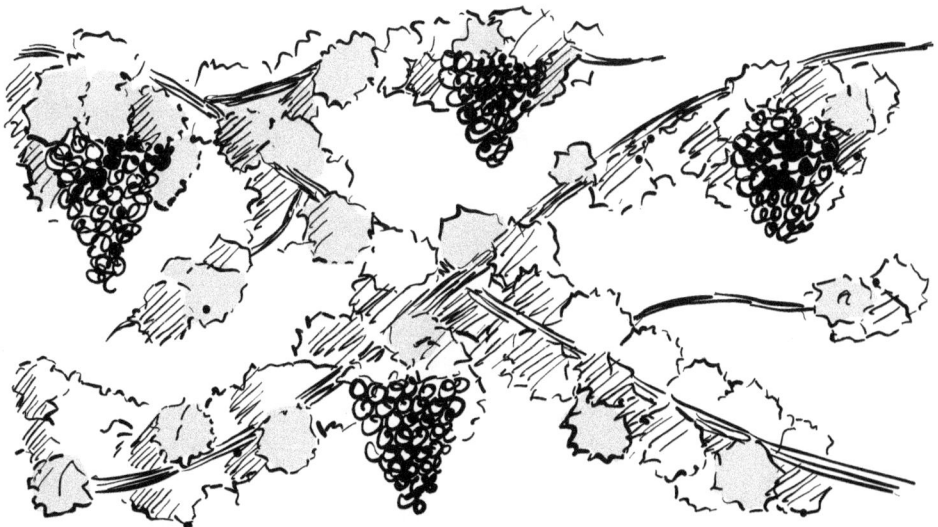

Music Notation

The Four Birds

David Lewis Stein, Alison Stein, Benjamin Stein   Benjamin Stein

VERSES 1-3

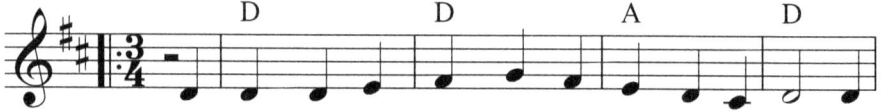

I went out one morn-ing, and what did I see?
The first sang of light at the start of the day, the
The third sang of night,_ of love and of play, the

Four might-y birds_ in four might-y trees, and they
next sang of work_ and bus - tle and play,
last sang of dreams that light - en the way,

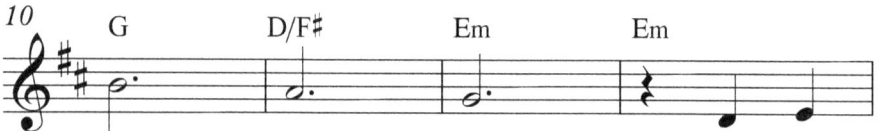

sang to me, and they

sang to me.

VERSES 4-5

And I said, we have wait - ed for e - ver and
We must stay in these trees, this is where we be -

2

e-ver, for you— to sing— your songs to -
long, but for you, all our voic-es may join in one

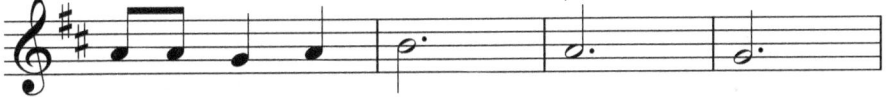

ge-ther, and they sang   to   me,
song, and they sang,   to   me,

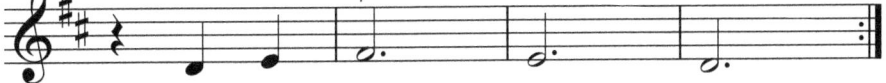

and they sang   to   me:
and they sang   to   me

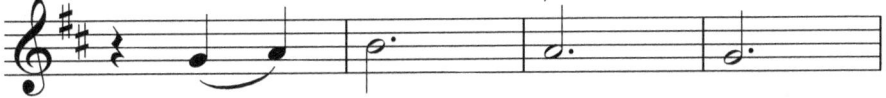

one—   might - y   song,

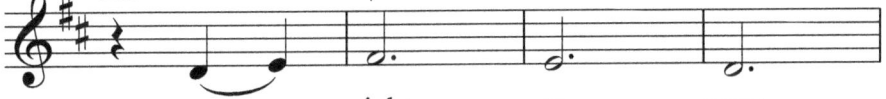

one—   might - y   song

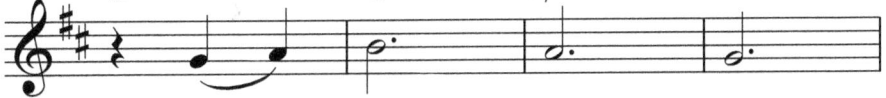

to——   lift   me   up,

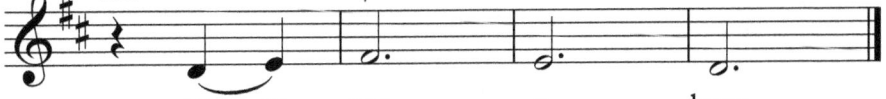

car - ry   me   a - long.

I Love to Tell the Story

K. Hankey, adapted.

W. G. Fischer

We love to tell the sto - ry, for those who know it

best seem hun-ger-ing and thirst-ing to_ hear it, like the

rest.   And   when,   in scenes of   glo - ry,   we

sing   the new, new_ song,   'twill   be   the old, old

sto - ry   that   we   have loved   so long.

Go Down, Moses

Trad. African American Spiritual

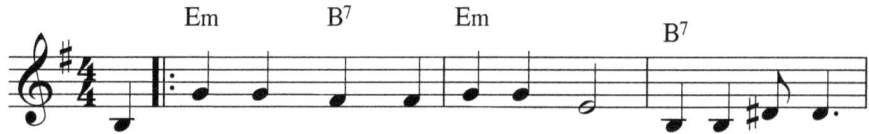

When Is - rael was in E-gypt land, Let my peo-ple
God told Mo - ses what to do,
Is - rael reached the wa-ter side,

go. Op - pressed so hard they could not stand;
To lead his peo - ple right on through;
Com - mand - ed God, "It may di - vide",

Let my peo-ple go. Go down, Mo-ses,

way down in E - gypt land. Tell_ old_____

Pha - roah, Let my peo-ple Go So
When

Dayenu

Alison/David Stein

Trad. Hebrew Tune

C   G

1.Had we on - ly fruit and trees,___
2.Could we scan the stars a - bove and
3.Could we live through books on shelves and
4.Could we on - ly ba - nish sor - row,
5.Could we on - ly join our voi - ces,

2   C   G

1.grain to plant, and fruit - ful trees,___
2.ne - ver feel the power of love,___
3.ne - ver come to know our - selves___
4.wipe our tears and face to - mor - row,
5.join our hands and share our choi - ces

3   C   G   C   G   C G C

1.grain to plant, and fruit - ful trees,_ da - ye - nu.
2.ne - ver feel the power of love,_
3.ne - ver come to know our selves_
4.wipe our tears and face to - mor - row,
5.join our hands and share our choi - ces

56

Da, da - ye - nu   Da, da - ye - nu

Da, da - ye - nu, da - ye - nu, da - ye - nu, da - ye - nu.

Da, da - ye - nu   Da, da - ye - nu

Da, da - ye - nu, da - ye - nu, da - ye - nu.

Were You There

Trad. African American Spiritual

Were you there when they nailed him to the tree?
Were you there when they laid him in the tomb?

Were you there when they nailed him to the
Were you there when they laid him in the

tree?_____ Oh,_____ some-times it
tomb?

caus - es me to trem-ble, trem-ble, trem-ble.

16

F   E⁷   Am

Were you there when they
Were you there when they

18

Dm   G⁷   C   F   C

nailed him to the tree?
laid him in the tomb?

Hope is the Answer

Alison and David Lewis Stein

Benjamin Stein

Hope is the an - swer, love is the way to build__ the bridge we have start-ed to - day. The road may be long, but we won't be de - feat-ed, we'll treat the whole world as we would be treated. Hope is the an - swer, love is the way to build__ the bridge we have start-ed to - day.

60

Hinei Ma Tov

Traditional Hebrew

Hi-nei ma tov u-ma na - yim she-vet a-

chim gam ya - chad   Hi - nei ma -

tov she-vet a-chim gam ya - chad   Hi-nei ma

tov u-ma na - yim   she-vet a-chim gam ya -

chad. Hi - nei ma-tov u - ma na - yim

she-vet a-chim gam ya-chad   Hi - nei ma tov u -

2

30
Cm Cm Bb Cm

ma na-yim she-vet a-chim gam ya-chad Hi nei ma

33
F Cm Bb

tov, hi-nei_ ma - tov, li_ li li_ li_ li_

36
Cm F Cm

li Hi nei ma-tov, hi-nei_ ma - tov, li_

39
Bb Cm Eb

li li_ li_ li_ li Hi - nei ma-tov u -

42
Bb Eb Bb

ma na-yim li_ li li_ li_ li

45
Cm Bb

nei ma - tov u - ma na-yim, hi -

47
F Cm

nei ma - tov u - ma na -yim.

I'll Sing You One-O

Alison/David Stein

Trad. Folk Song

Bb

I'll sing you one - o,
I'll sing you two - o,

Bb F Bb Bb

ALL SING TO-GE-THER NOW! What is your one - o?
What is your two - o?

Bb

One for the One who made it all,
Two,_____ two the tab - lets,

F Bb

one for the one who heard the call.
two for the two great tea - chers.

1.
Bb Eb F Bb

Me for you and you for me, sing-ing all to-ge-ther.

8 (2.) Bb
One for the One who made it all,

9 F / Bb
one for the one who heard the call.

10 Bb / Eb / F / Bb
Me for you and you for me, sing-ing all to-ge-ther.

12 Bb / Bb F / Bb
I'll sing you three-o, ALL SING TO-GE-THER NOW!

14 Bb / Bb F / C7 / F
What is your three-o? Three, three the fa - thers,

3

17 B♭   F   C⁷   F   B♭   E♭

Three, three, the tri - ni - ty.   Two, two, the tab-lets,

20 C⁷   F

two   for   the   two   great   tea - chers.

21 B♭   E♭

One   for   the   One   that   made   it   all

22 C⁷   F

One   for   the   one   that   heard   the   call

23 B♭   E♭   F   B♭

Me for you and you for me, sing-ing all to-ge-ther.

I'll sing you four - o, ALL SING TO-GE-THER NOW!
I'll sing you five - o,
I'll sing you six - o,
I'll sing you seven-o,

Repeat this section as the song continues,
counting backwards from each new
number; five to four, six to five to four, etc.

What is your four - o? Four for the gos-pel writ - ers,
What is your five - o? Five for the books of To - rah,
What is your six - o? Six for the days of mak - ing,
What is your seven-o? Seven for the day we all love best,

four   for   the   four   great   mo   -   thers.
Five   for   the   five   great   saints.
Six   for   the   six   great   a   -   ges.
Seven   for   the   day   we   get   to   rest.

Three, three the fa - thers, Three, three, the tri - ni-ty.

34 Bb / Eb / C⁷ / F

Two, two, the tab - lets, two for the two great tea - chers.

36 Bb / Eb

One for the One that made it all,

37 C⁷ / F

One for the one that heard the call,

38 Bb / Eb

Me for you and you for me,

LAST TIME ONLY: AND

39 F / Bb

sing - ing all to - ge - ther.

E - VER MORE SHALL BE - O!

O Canada

Robert Stanley Weir, adapted.

Calixa Lavallée

O Ca - na - da, our home and na-tive land.

True pa - triot love in all of us com mand. With

glow - ing hearts, we___ see thee rise, the___

true north strong and free. From far and wide, o___

Ca - na-da, we stand on guard for___ thee

God keep our land glo - rious and free.

O Ca - na - da, we stand on guard for thee!

O Ca - na - da, we stand on guard for thee!

Appendix

1.How did the Haggadah come to be?

The Haggadah began life as a prayer book for homeless people. At the beginning of the Common Era the Province of Judaea rebelled three times against the oppressive Roman Empire. The Romans considered even Jesus such a threat to their power they nailed him to a cross.

The Emperor Hadrian crushed the final Jewish rebellion and destroyed the temple in Jerusalem. Jews were scattered around the Mediterranean but these stiff necked people were determined to keep their faith alive. They took rituals that had been performed at the temple in Jerusalem and adapted them for prayer services in synagogues that spread around the world. The celebration of the exodus from Egypt was originally part of the synagogue service but in the Middle Ages, Jews began to expand portions that were celebrated in the home and codified them as the Haggadah, the "telling," much like the Haggadah we are using now.

So tonight with blessings and prayers, with recitation and singing, we tell the story of Moses leading the Jewish slaves out of Egypt and we tell the story of Christ's mission in Galilee and His crucifixion.

We share the traditional Passover feast with components that invoke historic memories and we end the evening with songs, blessings and sharing our hopes for the future.

2. How can we prepare a Passover Seder?

The Seder is essentially a festive meal built around the telling of the Exodus story and tonight, around the story of Christ's mission in Galilee.

Observant Jews who wish to experience the full, purifying commitment to Passover remove all bread and leavened products, from their home. They eat only matzos, unleavened wafers for eight days. They cook and serve the Passover feast on utensils and plates that have been ritually purified or kept apart and used only at Passover.

We leave it to participants in this Seder meal to choose how closely they wish to adhere to traditional preparations.

We are concerned here with what happens around the feast itself.

For this, some essential items must be on the table:

- Bowls of lightly salted water and there should be one bowl for every six or so people
- A candle for every six guests
- Plates of matzah
- Sufficient potatoes, and segments of orange for each guest
- Wine or non-alcoholic juice, at least enough for four glasses per person
- Eggs and vegetables or fruit fresh from the earth (parsley, watercress, potatoes or even strawberries will be fine) to be available for guests during the introductions about the Seder Plate

The plate designated as a "Seder plate" should have these components

- A roasted bone, preferably from lamb but a chicken bone will do
- A peeled hard-boiled egg slightly browned in a skillet pan ahead of time
- A bitter herb, usually horseradish, called maror, in Hebrew
- Charoseth, a sweet mixture of honey, wine, apples and nuts
- An orange or orange segment
- A sprig of parsley or watercress

The basic structure of the Seder, which we are following here, has been fixed over centuries of use. But over the years, people have made their own individual additions to the basic service in order to make the Seder an instructive and enjoyable experience. We offer here some of the ways our family and friends help celebrate Passover. We have even included a couple of favorite recipes. These are only suggestions but we hope that they will be helpful to people.

On the Table

- The table should be set in a joyful, spring like way - colourful napkins, attractive hors d'oeuvre dishes, and small pots of flowers such as African violets or primroses. Guests often take the little flower pots away with them at the end of the party
- For every guest, a setting of cutlery, both a dinner plate and a breakfast plate on top of the dinner plate, a wine glass, a water glass and a napkin. One person requires matches for lighting the candle
- Water pitchers and wine bottles
- Wine or non-alcoholic juice, at least enough for four glasses per person
- A copy of the Haggadah for every participant

The evening

Call people to come at least half an hour before you plan to begin reading the Haggadah so that they can begin to leave their daily cares aside and enter into a Passover/Easter frame of mind.

If a number of the guests are not familiar with each other one can designate one or two people to act as hosts to greet people and help them to feel at ease with each other. It is important to welcome the children in a happy, inviting way.
It can take two hours from the commencement of the reading of the Haggadah until the dinner begins so we have always offered guests something to snack on as they arrive—matzah crackers, tam-tams with pate and/or chopped liver.
The recitation of the Haggadah and the dinner itself can take three hours or longer, so it can be a good idea to start early. Some years, we began reading and reciting the Haggadah at 3 in the afternoon if there were young children among the participants.

We wanted the children to experience the Seder but we were concerned that this long evening not become an ordeal for them, so we made sure that toys and books and activities were available. You could include crayons and invite children to color their Haggadahs. Some years we had a baby sitter on hand. The sitter allowed the parents to participate more freely in the proceedings.

The dinner

Chicken and lamb are favorites but in some years we also included cold poached salmon. The Seder can be an opportunity for those who enjoy cooking to show off their skills. The Seder should be a dinner that people look forward to.

These are three favorite recipes:

Kate McQuiggan's Herb Roasted Chicken

Preheat oven to 400F
3 1/2 lb. Chicken
2 cloves garlic, squished
2 tbsp. lemon juice
1 tbsp. olive oil
1 tsp. Italian seasoning, crumbled (or any other herb mixture you like)
1 tsp. salt
¼ tsp. pepper
In small bowl combine all the seasonings. With a pastry brush, spread this mixture all over the chicken, inside and out. Place the chicken in a shallow roasting pan, preferably on a small rack so that the chicken won't sit in the drippings.
Roast uncovered for 20 minutes. If there are sufficient drippings at the bottom of the pan, scoop them up with a shallow spoon and baste the chicken with it.

If not, then pour some more olive oil in the bowl in which you mixed the seasonings and baste the chicken with that.
Continue to roast the chicken for one hour, basting it with drippings every 20 minutes.

N.B. To Roast Poultry:
– cook it at 400F for 15 minutes for every pound plus an extra 15 minutes cooking time
– if the chicken is stuffed, count stuffing as an extra pound
– therefore: 3 ½ lb requires approximately 1 hour & 8 minutes; 1.7kg = 3.75 lb requires approximately 1 hour & 15 minutes

Golda Teversham's Brisket

4-6 lb. brisket
2-5 onions, quartered/sliced
4-5 medium carrots
2 pkg. onion soup mix
1 ½ cup ketchup (for slightly less sweetness, reduce ketchup to 1 cup)
3 -5 tsp. minced garlic

Boil carrots and onions in small amount of water for 5 to 10 minutes. Remove with slotted spoon and reserve the water.

Mix the remaining ingredients together into a paste.
Place the brisket in a roasting pan (fat side down) and coat the top with the paste.
Cover the top with the vegetables. Place one cup of the reserved vegetable water in the pan around the brisket. Cover the pan with tin foil.
Bake in the oven at 200F for 8 hours.
Check after 4 hours. If the pan is looking dry add extra water.
NB: for a 2 lb. brisket cook 5 to 6 hours.

Carole Garber's Chocolate Pesach Cake

Separate 12 eggs and beat whites with a half cup of sugar until stiff.
Beat yolks with 1 cup of sugar until light yellow.
Fold 2 cups finely ground walnuts mixed with 3 teaspoons of potato starch into the yolk mixture.
Add ½ teaspoon of vanilla.
Chop 7 squares of semi-sweet chocolate and melt chocolate carefully and slowly.
Allow chocolate to cool to room temperature and mix in with yolk mixture.
Fold whites into yolk mixture SLOWLY.
Bake 45 minutes at 350 degrees F. in a large tube pan or you can use a 9 X 13 in. pan - not nearly as elegant.

3. If you are trying to build on a traditional Seder, shouldn't it be in Hebrew?

That is a difficult question.

The story is told of two rabbis, we will call, "Bill" and "Bob."
Rabbi Bill said only the Hebrew language can express the passion of Jewish prayer. So the Passover can only properly be celebrated in Hebrew. Rabbi Bob said many Jews living outside of Israel are not fluent in Hebrew. They sometimes repeat Hebrew prayers they could not express in their everyday language. Most non-Jews don`t know Hebrew at all. Rabbi Bob argued that people should pray in the language they are at home in.

They argued for years and finally Rabbi Bill grew exasperated and cried out, "Enough already! God, please tell Rabbi Bob that I am right."
The sky began to glow, a sweet fragrance of flowers filled the air and a gentle voice came from on high saying, "Rabbi Bill is right!"
Rabbi Bob was not impressed.

"We are not meant to appeal to a higher authority," he said. "God gave us the To-rah generations ago and He didn`t tell us to come back for clarifications. We have to work out these problems for ourselves. That`s what we`ve been doing all these years with the Talmud and all the great teachers, Rashi and Maimonides and the Bal Shem Tov, Moses Mendelssohn, Menachem Mendel Schneerson, and so many other wise and devoted teachers of the Torah."

So Rabbi Bill and Rabbi Bob went on arguing about the importance of Hebrew in the Passover Seder. As for the authors of this Haggadah, we come down fearlessly in favor of both camps.

We have set out the body of this work in English believing this would be most useful to people using this Haggadah. But for those who want more of the flavor of Hebrew we have included some Hebrew text with English transliterations.
If participants feel comfortable interpolating more Hebrew sections, please go ahead. Our feelings wouldn`t be hurt. Indeed we would be very pleased.

This Haggadah is meant to be only a beginning; we hope people will add to it, amend it, and shape it to their needs. The celebration of Passover is a work in progress.

4. What's with the questions that invite people to keep interrupting the service with?

At a traditional Seder the importance of educating children is paramount. Older people at the table pay careful attention to questions raised by the younger participants and treat their comments with respect. Isn't asking questions essential for learning? Didn't Jesus rebuke his disciples when they tried to keep a crowd of questioning children away from him?

Doesn't the Passover Haggadah deal with four kinds of questioning children: The wise child, the indifferent child, the angry child and the ignorant child?

Doesn't questioning power the Talmud, that vast study of how to lead a religious life when all around you people are going off in other directions?

Didn't Socrates think asking questions is the way to reach the truth and hasn't much of the methodology of classical Greek philosophy been absorbed into the framework of Christian theology?

Didn't even Karl Marx argue that resolving historical questions through the dialectical process would lead finally to a materialist utopia?

Why does a Jew always answer a question by asking another question?

So we hope people participating in this Seder will feel free to pose questions of their own and challenge the answers.

To help them along, we have marked with a star places where we think questions can begin.   *

5. Who says what… and when …during the Seder?

In some families, one person reads the entire Haggadah we have laid out here. Some families go to the other extreme with people speaking a sentence or two, reciting the whole Haggadah in a round robin style.
There is no universally recognized precedent for reciting the Haggadah.
In this case, we have suggested the service be led by a conductor who calls on participants for dramatic effect at significant moments.

We leave it to the people taking part in the Seder to choose formats that work best for them. But we do offer a couple of small suggestions. Sometimes with friends we told the story of Moses as a round robin with a person stopping in the middle of a sentence and even in the middle of a word, and leaving it to the next person to pick up. Mistakes were often made that inspired corrections and good natured laughter. On other occasions we divided people into small groups and gave them cards with significant events… Moses parting the Red Sea, Jesus walking on the water. Participants were required to act out these events and others had to guess what the actors were doing.

Such innovations may sound irreverent and even childish but in practice they helped people to appreciate nuances of the Passover and Easter stories. They also helped to break up a service that can often carry on for over an hour or two before the full meal is served. The Seder is a serious occasion but it doesn't have to be a somber one.

6. How far can people go with an interfaith Haggadah? A personal witness:

How can observant Jews allow even a few alterations in the Seder service without being driven to keep on making changes until Passover becomes only a wordy ceremony, empty of the power to move people?

How can passionate Christians who believe they possess the One Truth that leads to eternal life refrain from pressing that truth on people who do not share their faith? Definitive answers to these questions we do not have. We can only draw on our own experience.

For many years, David attended Saturday morning services at Shaarei Tzedec, a small synagogue that observed a strictly Orthodox form of service. He was drawn by the spiritual power of the cantor, Sholem Langner, leading the congregation in singing the traditional Sabbath prayers. Shaarei Tzedec was in downtown Toronto but it could have fitted easily into the Poland of a century earlier. Other members of the congregation knew that David was not an observant Jew and that Alison was not even Jewish. But they accepted us both as part of their community.

We came to believe that people who are secure in their own religious observances do not feel threatened by praying beside those who do not share the depth of their faith.

On Sunday mornings, David and Alison went together to the Metropolitan Community Church of Toronto. The network of Metropolitan Community Churches is a home for lesbian, gay, bisexual and transgender people as well as for traditionally heterosexual people like David and Alison. They first visited MCCT because their daughter Kate's dear friend, Paul Fairley, who was like a member of their own family, had become an MCC deacon and then a minister.

They came to MCCT as visitors but stayed on to become part of the congregation. Alison, who had been raised in the United Church, a Canadian amalgamation of Methodist and Presbyterian churches, and later became an Anglican convert, felt at home with the MCCT service. David looked into the faces of people around him and saw strength that grew from their struggles to lead open, honest lives. David thought, "I want to be with these people. I can grow in spirit praying with these people."

David was concerned though that they might think he was a potential convert to Christianity. David is proudly Jewish. So he began to wear a yarmulke, the traditional Jewish skull cap, to Sunday services at the Metropolitan Community Church. Brent Hawkes, the pastor of MCCT, asked David to get more yarmulkes and he placed them at the back of the church for other people to use. Brent Hawkes has been an important person for Alison and David. During services, when the time comes for communion, David crosses his arms in front of him as a sign that he does not take the wafer or the wine but is there for a blessing.

People sometimes ask David how he can accept a blessing in a Christian church. David can only tell them, "I'll take a blessing anywhere I can get one."
Those experiences have helped form the thinking of this Haggadah.
We hope people will add their own experiences and make this Haggadah their own spiritual experience.

ℰcknowledgements

In preparing *First Seder/ Last Supper* we read and studied these Haggadahs. We would not wish to imply that these authors would support and endorse what we have written but we certainly appreciated and enjoyed the work that they have done.

Haggadah Sources
Aigen, Rabbi Ronald. Wellsprings of Freedom. Marquis (Montreal), 2012.
Anisfeld, Rabbi Sharon Cohen, Tara Mohr & Catherine Spector. The Women's Seder Sourcebook. Jewish Lights Publishing (Woodstock, Vermont), 2003.
Ben-Khayyim, Dr. Dov. The Telling: A Loving Haggadah for Passover. Rakhamim Publications (Berkeley), 1989.
Broner, E.M., with Naomi Nimrod. The Women's Haggadah. HarperSanFrancisco, A Division of HarperCollinsPublications (New York), 1993, 1994.
Elwell, Sue Levi. The Open Door, A Passover Haggadah. Central Conference of American Rabbis (New York), 2002.
Friedland, Jacqueline. A Women's Seder. Miles Nadal J.C.C. (Toronto), 2005.
Kalechofsky, Roberta. Haggadah for the Liberated Lamb. Micah Publications (Marblehead, Mass.), 2002.
Kaplan, Mordecai M., Eugene Kohn & Ira Eisenstein. The New Haggadah. Behrman House Inc. (West Orange, NJ.), 1942, 1978.
Klein, Mordell. Passover. Keter Books (Jerusalem), 1973.
Levitt, Rabbi Joy & Rabbi Michael Strassfeld. A Night of Questions, a Passover Haggadah. The Reconstructionist Press (Elkins Park, Penn.), 2000.
Rabinowicz, Rachel Anne. Passover Haggadah, the Feast of Freedom. The Rabbinical Assembly (USA), 1982.
Sacks, Rabbi Jonathon. Rabbi Jonathon Sack's Haggadah. Continuum (New York), 2010.
Schecter, Ellen. The Family Haggadah. Viking, Penguin Group (New York), 1999.
Shahn, Ben & Cecil Roth. Ben Shahn's Haggadah. Little, Brown & Co.(Boston), 1965.
Silberman, Shoshana. A Family Haggadah II. Kar-Ben Publishing (Minneapolis), 1997.
Wiesel, Elie. A Passover Haggadah. A Touchstone Book, Simon& Schuster, Inc (New York), 1993.
Zion, Noam & David Dishon. A Different Night, the Family Participation Haggadah. The Diker Centre. The Shalom Hartman Institute (Jerusalem& Englewood, NJ), 1997.

Other Sources
Armstrong, Karen. The Great Transformation, The Beginning of our Religious Traditions. Alfred A. Knopf (Toronto), 2006.
Armstrong, Karen. Twelve Steps to a Compassionate Life. Alfred A. Knopf (Toronto), 2010.
Kaplan, Aryeh. Jewish Meditation, A Practical Guide. Schocken Books (New York), 1985.
Swami Sivananda, Radha. Kundalini, Yoga for the West. Timeless Books (Spokane, WA), 1978.
Vardey, Lucinda (ed.) God in All Worlds, An Anthology of Contemporary Spiritual Writing. Alfred A. Knopf Canada (Toronto), 1995.

Celebrations of Passover are a collective experience and we would like to particularly thank these people who have been involved in the evolution of this Haggadah: Our children, and their partners and the grandchildren who have inspired, spurred and supported us — Annika, Griffin and Arden, Benjamin, Christine and Hannah, Kate, Mark, Emma and Daniel

Members of our chosen Seder Family who over the years since 1965 have come together for Seders: Martin Stone, Larry and Carole Garber, Jennifer Garber, Fiona McCool, Belle Garber, Sam Garber, Marian Hebb, Otto Siebenmann, Sara Hebb, Paul and Matthieu Dupré, Harve Sokoloff, Paul Sokoloff, Gloria Bryan, Cassandra, Adrian and Shane Bryan Sokoloff, Laraine Herzog, Erna Paris, Tom Robinson, Michelle Paris, Roland Paris, Sarah Hunter, Ben Hunter, Guy Hunter, Andrea Holtslander, Sam Hunter, Eleanor, Rebecca and Naomi Hart, Chris Currie, Lene Currie, Graham Currie, Marilyn Powell, Yael Schacter, Greg Beilis, Benjamin Beilis, Zoe Beilis, Marvyn Novick, Gillian Novick, Nat Paul, Ezra Paul, Sacha Paul, Janie Romoff, Lisa Robichaud, Maxine Sidran, Tess MacKenzie

Brent Hawkes, the senior pastor of Metropolitan Community Church of Toronto who has hosted inter-faith Seders and truly made MCCT "A House of Prayer for All People", the reverend Deana Dudley and deacons Sandra Millar and Linda Leenders who organized the Seders at MCCT where this Haggadah was allowed to breathe

Lorraine Kirchmann, Judy Sarick, Marian Hebb, Mary Sue McCarthy and the Arnprior Christian Meditation Group for discussion and ideas

Our production team: copy editor Heather Lang and consultants, Oren Berman and Chris Sansom

And a special thanks to our creative team: Colin White, who designed the book and drew the illustrations and Ben Stein who made the music for this book.

About the Authors

Alison Stein is a Christian, a student of Yoga and eastern religions. She has been a dancer, a member of a children's acting company, a theatre director, a guidance councillor, a teacher in London and Paris and for many years taught dramatic arts in the schools of suburban Toronto.

David Lewis Stein is Jewish. For many years he was the municipal affairs columnist for the Toronto Star and he has been a journalist in London, Paris and New York. He has taught urban affairs at the University of Toronto. He is the author of three novels, three books on politics, a collection of short stories, a stage play and several radio plays.

David and Alison have celebrated many seasons of Passover and Easter with family and friends. This book grows out of those happy times.

Clink Street Publishing
United Kingdom
Copyright
Text by Alison & David Lewis Stein
Original music by Benjamin Stein

www.ingramcontent.com/pod-product-compliance
Lightning Source LLC
Chambersburg PA
CBHW071906020426
42331CB00010B/2699